A..imal Farm

Animal Farm by George Orwell is an exciting and unusual story, but it is also a story with a strong political purpose. In this study book, you will explore the motives behind the author's writing and investigate how and why *Animal Farm* has come to be regarded as a classic of its kind. You will also be developing your skills as:

SPEAKERS AND LISTENERS

by reading and discussing sections of the text with others
by working together to unfold the meaning of the story
by forming and voicing your own opinions on key themes

READERS

by sharing first impressions in order to make comparisons and connections
by reading and re-reading closely to develop your understanding
by exploring the different ways writers use language to convey meaning and
   attitude

WRITERS

by making notes and writing commentaries
by writing imaginatively in response to some of the extracts
by using writing in a range of styles and for a variety of audiences
by writing more formally for a coursework assignment

1

GEORGE ORWELL

George Orwell was born in 1903. After leaving
school he served in the Indian Imperial Police in
Burma. In 1936 he went to Spain to fight for the
Republicans in the Spanish Civil War. In the
passage below, from an essay published in 1946
called 'Why I Write', he recalls how these
experiences affected and inspired his work.

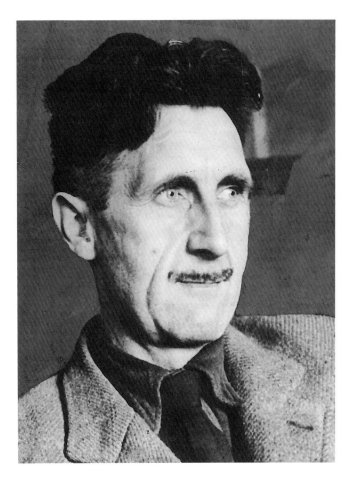

In a peaceful age I might have written ornate or
merely descriptive books, and might have
remained almost unaware of my political loyalties.
As it is I have been forced into becoming a sort of
pamphleteer. First I spent five years in an
unsuitable profession (the Indian Imperial Police,
in Burma), and then I underwent poverty and the
sense of failure. This increased my natural hatred
of authority and made me for the first time fully
aware of the existence of the working class, and
the job in Burma had given me some
understanding of the nature of imperialism: but
these experiences were not enough to give me an
accurate political orientation. Then came Hitler,
the Spanish Civil War, etc. By the end of 1935 I
had still failed to reach a firm decision.

The Spanish Civil War and other events in
1936–7 turned the scale and thereafter I knew
where I stood. Every line of serious work that I
have written since 1936 has been written, directly
or indirectly, *against* totalitarianism and *for*
democratic Socialism, as I understand it. It seems
to me nonsense, in a period like our own, to think
that one can avoid writing of such subjects.
Everyone writes of them in one guise or another. It
is simply a question of which side one takes and
what approach one follows.

When I sit down to write a book, I do not say to
myself, 'I am going to produce a work of art.' I
write it because there is some lie that I want to
expose, some fact to which I want to draw
attention, and my initial concern is to get a
hearing. But I could not do the work of writing a
book, or even a long magazine article, if it were
not also an aesthetic experience.

Animal Farm was the first book in which I tried,
with full consciousness of what I was doing, to
fuse political and artistic purpose into one whole.

Orwell died in 1950. *Animal Farm*, published in 1945, and his novel
Nineteen Eighty-Four, published in 1949, made him world-famous.

HELP

READING LOG

You may find it useful to have an exercise book to record your thoughts and feelings as you study the novel. Use it from time to time to write down things you don't understand or find interesting, your feelings about the main characters or to note questions that come to your mind. These notes will be useful later on when you do some extended writing about the novel. Remember to record page or chapter numbers with your notes to make going back to them easy. Use your journal to 'think on paper'.

Animal Farm is an unusual story in that it is an animal story written for adults. Whilst it is possible to read *Animal Farm* simply as a story about animals it has another level of meaning. This makes the story an **allegory**.

> **Allegory** is a way of writing a story so that it has two different, but coherent, meanings. The first is the clear literal meaning on the story's surface; the second is a hidden, deeper meaning or message.

George Orwell has used animal characters as a way of making a point about human behaviour. In an allegory human behaviour can be simplified and so becomes clearer. Often the process of simplifying something leads to an exaggeration of certain aspects of that behaviour. This helps the reader to identify what exactly the writer is criticising. The use of animals as characters allows the reader to stand back and be detached from the criticisms, even though they can work out that it is directed at all humans. The world which initially seemed so different to ours quickly becomes recognisable!

There are many other stories which are written as allegory, for example, *Aesop's Fables.*

- Do you remember the story-line of any of *Aesop's Fables?* 'The Hare and the Tortoise' is possibly one of the best-known. Read the story on the following page and discuss with a partner what is being said about aspects of human behaviour.

THE HARE AND THE TORTOISE

The Hare was once boasting of his speed before the other animals. 'I have never yet been beaten,' said he, 'when I put forth my full speed. I challenge any one here to race with me.'

The Tortoise said quietly, 'I accept your challenge.'

'That is a good joke,' said the Hare; 'I could dance round you all the way.'

'Keep your boasting till you're beaten,' answered the Tortoise. 'Shall we race?'

So a course was fixed and a start was made. The Hare darted almost out of sight at once, but soon stopped and, to show his contempt for the Tortoise, lay down to have a nap. The Tortoise plodded on and plodded on, and when the Hare awoke from his nap, he saw the Tortoise just near the winning-post and could not run up in time to save the race. Then said the Tortoise:

'Plodding wins the race.'

FIRST IMPRESSIONS

The novel opens with a memorable description of Farmer Jones of Manor
Farm and then immediately sets the stage for the action which is to follow.
Read the first two paragraphs of *Animal Farm:*

Mr Jones, of the Manor Farm, had locked the hen-houses for the night, but was too drunk to remember to shut the pop-holes. With the ring of light from his lantern dancing from side to side, he lurched across the yard, kicking off his boots at the back door, drew himself a last glass of beer from the barrel in the scullery, and made his way up to bed, where Mrs Jones was already snoring.

As soon as the light in the bedroom went out there was a stirring and a fluttering all through the farm buildings. Word had gone round during the day that Old Major, the prize Middle White boar, had had a strange dream on the previous night and wished to communicate it to the other animals. It had been agreed that they should all meet in the big barn as soon as Mr Jones was safely out of the way. Old Major (so he was always called, though the name under which he had been exhibited was Willingdon Beauty) was so highly regarded on the farm that everyone was quite ready to lose an hour's sleep in order to hear what he had to say.

- Discuss with a partner how George Orwell has tried to capture your attention at the very beginning of this story. Write a list of the points you discuss.

- Write down the words and the phrases which Orwell uses to describe:

  1 Farmer Jones   2 Old Major

What contrasting impressions does he establish by using these particular words?

- How does Orwell create an atmosphere of excitement and anticipation? How does he make you want to read on?

Now read the rest of Chapter 1.

I HAVE A DREAM

In Chapter 1, Old Major speaks eloquently to the animals. He reminds them of the ways in which they are oppressed and exploited by the farmer, Mr Jones. Here is a short extract from his speech (which you need to read carefully in full):

'No animal in England is free. The life of an animal is misery and slavery: that is the plain truth.

   But is this simply part of the order of nature? Is it because this land of ours is so poor that it cannot afford a decent life to those who dwell upon it? No, comrades, a thousand times no! The soil of England is fertile, its climate is good, it is capable of affording food in abundance to an enormously greater number of animals than now inhabit it. This single farm of ours would support a dozen horses, twenty cows, hundreds of sheep – all of them living in a comfort and a dignity that are now almost beyond our imagining. Why then do we continue in this miserable condition? Because nearly the whole of the produce of our labour is stolen from us by human beings. There, comrades, is the answer to all our problems. It is summed up in a single word – Man. Man is the only real enemy we have. Remove Man from the scene, and the root cause of hunger and overwork is abolished for ever.'

Like many other great leaders, Old Major uses a speech to do two things:
1 To put forward his ideas and his vision.
2 To communicate directly to his audience and thus attempt to convince them by the power of his **oratory**.

Oratory is inspired, often passionate, public speaking. An 'orator' uses techniques such as:

asking rhetorical questions – *But is this simply the order of nature?*

repeating key words and phrases – *a dozen horses, twenty cows, hundreds of sheep*

appealing directly to the audience – *No, comrades, a thousand times no!*

Great oratory can help to overcome tyranny, and put in words the hopes, dreams and fears of millions – it can sometimes change the world.

Not all orators use their way with words for the common good, however. Adolf Hitler was undoubtedly a great speaker, yet used this power to release the huge destructive force of Nazism and the Holocaust. He fully recognised the power of oratory to achieve destructive as well as constructive goals:

'The force which ever set in motion the great historical avalanches of religious and political movements is the magic power of the spoken word. The broad masses of a population are more amenable to the appeal of rhetoric than to any other force'

Adolf Hitler writing in Mein Kampf

- Are Hitler's words as true in an age of television and the internet as they were earlier in the twentieth century?

- How do you think the animals in *Animal Farm* will react to Old Major's speech? Different animals will probably react in different ways. From what you find out about the different animals in Chapter 1, make brief notes on what they are likely to think and do as a result of listening to Old Major. Which animals would argue for an uprising? Which would not agree with Old Major? Which would suggest caution? Which would be fearful of change?

- Script a short dialogue between one of the following pairs of animals to show how they might react differently.

  Benjamin and a pig
  Boxer and Clover
  a dog and a hen

THE APPEAL OF RHETORIC

Look at these extracts from some famous speeches given by influential twentieth-century figures.

I have a dream that one day even the state of Mississippi, a desert state sweltering with the heat of injustice and oppression, will be transformed into an oasis of freedom and justice.

I have a dream that my four little children will one day live in a nation where they will not be judged by the color of their skin but by the content of their character.

I have a dream today.

I have a dream that one day the state of Alabama, whose governor's lips are presently dripping with the words of interposition and nullification, will be transformed into a situation where little black boys and black girls will be able to join hands with little white boys and white girls and walk together as sisters and brothers.

I have a dream today.

I have a dream that one day every valley shall be exalted, every hill and mountain shall be made low, the rough places will be made plains and the crooked places will be made straight, and the glory of the Lord shall be revealed, and all flesh shall see it together.

This is our hope.

Martin Luther King

If we look around in the world, where do we see women happy, well treated and satisfied unless where the world has been made what women wish it to be? Men are responsible if they allow the present condition of things to continue. Women have the power to work out their own salvation. But as it is, if a woman is ruined, if a child is injured, man is responsible for it all. It is a responsibility I would not care to have, and, as things are, I would not be a man for all the world. If women fail as men have failed, then they will bear the burden with them. But since men cannot protect and shield us, let us share the duty with them, let us use our power so that woman may be a participant, not to tyrannize over man but to take a share in the responsibilities of ruling, without which there is no real representative government. What we really are interested in in this fight is the uplifting of the sex and better conditions of humanity than men can secure . . . What we want is the combined intelligence of man and woman working for the salvation of the children of the race.

Emmeline Pankhurst

We have waited too long for our freedom! We can no longer wait. Now is the time to intensify the struggle on all fronts. To relax our efforts now would be a mistake which generations to come will not be able to forgive. The sight of freedom looming on the horizon should encourage us to redouble our efforts. It is only through disciplined mass action that our victory can be assured.

. . .

Our march to freedom is irreversible. We must not allow fear to stand in our way. Universal suffrage on a common voters' roll in a united, democratic and non-racial South Africa is the only way to peace and racial harmony.

. . .

I have fought against white domination and I have fought against black domination. I have cherished the ideal of a democratic and free society in which all persons live together in harmony and with equal opportunity. It is an ideal which I hope to live for and to achieve. But if needs be, it is an ideal for which I am prepared to die. *Amandla* (power)!

Nelson Mandela

We have before us an ordeal of the most grievous kind. We have before us many, many long months of struggle and of suffering. You ask, what is our policy? I will say: It is to wage war, by sea, land and air, with all our might and with all the strength that God can give us: to wage war against a monstrous tyranny, never surpassed in the dark, lamentable catalogue of human crime. That is our policy. You ask, What is our aim? I can answer in one word: Victory – victory at all costs, victory in spite of all terror, victory, however long and hard the road may be; for without victory, there is no survival. Let that be realized; no survival for the British Empire; no survival for all that the British Empire has stood for, no survival for the urge and impulse of the ages, that mankind will move forward towards its goal. But I take up my task with buoyancy and hope. I feel sure that our cause will not be suffered to fail among men. At this time I feel entitled to claim the aid of all, and I say, 'Come, then, let us go forward together with our united strength.'

Winston Churchill

- These speeches were often written but were only memorable because they were spoken. A speaker can combine words, voice and gesture in powerful ways. On a copy of the extracts, underline or highlight moments in each speech which appeal to the audience's emotions or feelings.

- With a partner, select a few lines from the speeches and practice different ways of saying them. Build in two or three gestures that add to the impact of the section you have chosen.

- Which of these four extracts do you find most compelling, most powerful? Prepare a short explanation as to why you have made your choice. Refer to both the content of the speech and the way that ideas and feelings are conveyed.

HELP

KEEPING TRACK OF THE STORY

It is very important for you to have a good understanding of the plot of this novel for your examination or coursework. It may be some time before you come back to revise your work. Use your reading log to compile a short plot summary for each chapter of the novel. A plot summary for Chapter 1 has been done for you below. Copy it out and add your own comments next to some of the points – two have been done for you. Your comments should be about details that you discuss or ideas you don't want to forget. Do this for each chapter and by the end of the book you will have a useful set of notes for revising for the examination.

PLOT SUMMARY: CHAPTER 1

Introduced to Mr Jones   *He is cruel to the animals and often drunk*

Animals arrive for Old Major's meeting,

Old Major explains his dream and gives his message

Taught 'Beasts of England'   *which is very optimistic about their future*

Singing awakes Mr Jones

Chapter 1 is very important because it contains Old Major's speech in which he explains that the animals are badly treated and have nothing to look forward to. Man, he says, is the cause of their misery and must be got rid of. However, this chapter is also important because it introduces several of the other animals.

Start to make notes about some of the farm animals. Give each character a page and add as many details as you can during your reading. Always remember to write down the page number for each detail and a useful quotation if possible.

| *Page 2* | *Boxer and Clover came in together ... setting down their vast hairy hoofs with great care ...* | *This shows how considerate they are. Makes them sound like a team.* |

Do this for the characters of Muriel, Benjamin and Mollie.

REVOLUTION!

Read Chapter 2, then look carefully again at the section which begins: 'Now, as it turned out, the Rebellion was achieved much earlier and more easily than anyone had expected' and ends '...and slept as they had never slept before.'

Write two reports about this incident for the local police. Write the first one as an animal of your choice. Write the second report from the point of view of Mr Jones. The two reports should contain the same factual details but the thoughts and feelings they express should be very different. You may find it helpful to begin by making a list of the points which you want to include. For example:

1 *The reasons why the animals revolted against Mr Jones*

2 *The details of how their revolution took place*

3 *The animals' feelings about it afterwards*

4 *How you imagine Mr Jones would feel about losing his farm*

The three main characters in Chapter 2 are Snowball, Napoleon and Squealer. Look carefully at the descriptions of these animals in this chapter, then answer the questions below.

Napoleon and Squealer as depicted in the 1954 animated film

- What are we told about them and how are they different?

- Start your notes for these three characters as you have done for the other characters you have met so far. Which of the following words would you use for which character? You may use more than one word for a character, or use a word more than once.

    ruthless   persuasive   inventive   determined   confusing   sharp

- Find evidence from Chapter 2 to back up your choice of words.

THE CHINESE CALENDAR

Animal Farm is based around a number of different animals who all have individual characters. The Chinese calendar is also based on animal characteristics which are used to signify characteristics in people depending on the year in which they were born.

The Chinese name each year after an animal. A legend says that the creatures concerned agreed to have a swimming race across a river to decide whose year should come first. The rat won because he cunningly jumped on the back of the ox, who was the best swimmer among them, and then leapt ashore at the last moment. There are twelve animals involved, their year coming round again in a regular cycle. As the legend suggests, each cycle starts with the Year of the Rat, followed by the ox, the tiger, the rabbit and so on. People are supposed to have the characteristics of the animal in whose year they were born. In recent times, the Year of the Rat has occurred in 1972, 1984 and 1996. Match up your date of birth with the Chinese calendar and the appropriate animal. What characteristics are **you** supposed to have?

The Pig Intelligent, but also emotional and easily upset.

The Rat Sleeps by day, searches for food at night: people born in daytime will have an easy life, those born at night will work hard.

The Dog Loyal, like the tiger, and quick to learn, like the monkey.

The Ox Patient and thoughtful, tries hard at things.

The Cock Proud, hard-working and ambitious.

The Tiger Loyal to friends and a provider for the family.

The Monkey Curious and quick to learn. Makes a good parent.

The Rabbit Happy and blessed with large family!

The Ram Proud, but good at leading and helping others.

The Dragon Likes to be alone and objects to change.

The Snake Wise and agile. Versatile and good at many things.

The Horse Strong and friendly, gets on well with strangers.

A **stereotype** is a person or thing about which there is a generally fixed and unchanging view. The characteristics given to the animals in the Chinese calendar could be described as 'stereotypical'.

- Are any of the characters of the animals in *Animal Farm* stereotypical? Discuss this with a partner.

- Copy the grid below and fill in the 'Description' column for each animal as you meet them in the novel. Do they live up to any stereotypes? If not, in what ways do they differ?

ANIMAL	DESCRIPTION	REPRESENTS
HORSES	*Intelligent creatures. Very useful to humans. Strong but can also be gentle. Easily trained. Dangerous if wild or bad.*	
PIGS		
SHEEP		
DOGS		
HENS		
CATS		

ANIMAL FARM AS AN ALLEGORY

Look back at page 3 for the details of what allegory means if you are unsure. Each animal group represents one group or type of humans. In Chapters 1 and 2 we have already seen the pigs start to take over and control what is happening on Animal Farm. We have seen that they are the most intelligent animals but they have also started to look after themselves more than the other animals, for example by taking the milk to drink. What different kinds of people are represented in this story by the different breeds of animals? Write your ideas in the box labelled 'Represents' under each animal group on your grid. For example, the horses could be said to represent the hard-working, loyal members of society.

- Write about the members of your family, discussing which Chinese Year they were born in and whether or not they appear to fit those characteristics. You might like to compare this with the characteristics of their astrological star sign. Use the library to find out more about each system.

- Investigate the presentation of two or more animal types as portrayed in children's cartoons on television.

SUMMER AND AUTUMN

Read Chapter 3 and then look closely at the following extract.

Boxer was the admiration of everybody. He had been a hard worker even in Jones's time, but now he seemed more like three horses than one; there were days when the entire work of the farm seemed to rest upon his mighty shoulders. From morning to night he was pushing and pulling, always at the spot where the work was hardest. He had made an arrangement with one of the cockerels to call him in the mornings half an hour earlier than anyone else, and would put in some volunteer labour at whatever seemed to be most needed, before the regular day's work began.

Motto: I will work harder!

- Discuss a possible motto for the other main characters. Support your choice of motto with a quotation from the book. You could illustrate this with a sketch of the character.

- In groups select one character each. You are going to be in the hot seat as if you are that character while the others in your group put questions to you. You need to try to answer as you think the character would have answered and reflect the feelings s/he might have had.

- Once this task has been completed, record in your journal how you felt as that character. What were you angry about? Who do you trust? Record as many details as you can.

THE PIGS

In Chapter 3 the differences between Napoleon and Snowball become more obvious.

The pigs also begin to use **propaganda** to persuade the other animals.

Propaganda is action or writing designed to spread particular ideas or opinions. It is designed to convince people of the opinions or views it supports. Propaganda often uses false or distorted information to persuade people to act or think in a particular way.

Read this speech by Squealer and then complete the task on the page opposite.

'You do not imagine, I hope, that we pigs are doing this in a spirit of selfishness and privilege? Many of us actually dislike milk and apples. I dislike them myself. Our sole object in taking these things is to preserve our health. Milk and apples (this has been proved by Science, comrades) contain substances absolutely necessary to the well-being of a pig. We pigs are brain-workers. The whole management and organisation of this farm depend on us. Day and night we are watching over your welfare. It is for your sake that we drink that milk and eat those apples. Do you know what would happen if we pigs failed in our duty? Jones would come back! Yes, Jones would come back! Surely, comrades . . . surely there is no one among you who wants to see Jones come back.'

1 Look back at the work you did on Old Major's speech on pages 6 and 7. In what ways is this speech by Squealer similar to that speech?

This speech by Squealer also includes the following techniques:

- He uses an **expert,** in this case Science to back up what he is saying. Notice that he doesn't actually explain what science has found out but simply refers to it knowing that his audience will believe in science. Why do you think Orwell used a capital letter for science?

- He uses the argument they might have used against him in order to **disprove their argument**: *'You do not imagine, I hope, that we pigs are doing this in a spirit of selfishness and privilege?'* In this way he voices their opinion for them and is then able to ridicule it.

- He **promotes the pigs** as selfless workers, working, even eating and drinking, for the good of everyone else. What does he say about the role of the pigs on the farm?

- He **threatens** the other animals with the return of Mr Jones. By using the one thing they are afraid of he knows that they will put up with a lot of other inequalities. *'Now if there was one thing that the animals were completely certain of, it was that they did not want Jones back.'*

2 At the beginning of Chapter 4 Mr Jones is said to be *'complaining to anyone who would listen of the monstrous injustice he had suffered in being turned out of his property...'* If Mr Jones really wanted to persuade people instead of just complain to them, how might he have done this?

- Write a speech for Mr Jones in which he attempts to persuade other farmers to help him get his farm back. Use a variety of the techniques you have identified in the two speeches in *Animal Farm.* (See the Help Box opposite for guidance). This could be used as a Speaking and Listening assessment.

3 Create a propaganda poster for Animal Farm. Think about a suitable slogan and how the illustrations might work to support it. The aim of the poster is to celebrate the achievements at Animal Farm as a way of encouraging the same action on other farms. It could do this by detailing the treatment of animals by humans.

On the next page is an example of a Russian propaganda poster from 1920. How does it convey its message?

HELP

TECHNIQUES ASSOCIATED WITH PROPAGANDA

Limited details – select only the facts which are helpful to you. Ignore everything else.

Rhetorical questions – which then supply the answer.

Opinion as fact – boldly state your opinion as if it is definite. It doesn't have to be true!

Repetition – to emphasise key feelings or to make others believe you if you say it often enough.

Identify the common enemy – often by threatening what they could do. Provide solidarity.

Spread false information – but make it sound believable.

- Start your speech, 'Fellow landowners . . .' as a way of trying to making the farmers think they have something in common and sounding friendly.

- Use the pronouns 'you', 'we' and 'they' most to emphasise farmers together against a common enemy.

- Repeat phrases.

- Ask rhetorical questions.

- Introduce the idea that rebellion at more farms will follow to scare the farmers into supporting you.

Before: One with the Plough, Seven with a Spoon

Now: He who does not Work shall not Eat

THE BATTLE OF THE COWSHED

Complete this section and group task **before** reading Chapter 4.

Jones and all his men, with half a dozen others from Foxwood and Pinchfield, had entered the five-barred gate and were coming up the cart-track that led to the farm. They were all carrying sticks, except Jones, who was marching ahead with a gun in his hands. Obviously they were going to attempt the recapture of the farm.

This had long been expected, and all preparations had been made. Snowball, who had studied an old book of Julius Caesar's campaigns which he had found in the farmhouse, was in charge of the defensive operations.

HELP

Use different colours for different strategies and groups of animals and draw arrows to show their direction of movement. Number the arrows to show the sequence of actions and movements. Devise a system of codes and sounds for communication between your forces and make sure all are clear about their role in the operation.

PLANNING A CAMPAIGN

- Work in small groups with one person in role as Snowball. Use the plan of the farmyard opposite to devise your own defensive strategy.

  Consider these questions:

  1 Where is the attack likely to come from?

  2 How many humans might be involved?

  3 How many animals are there on Animal Farm?

  4 What natural weapons do the animals have?

  5 What can those animals with no natural weapons do?

  6 Where will the animals be positioned?

  7 Who will do what and when?

  8 Do you have a range of strategies in case your attackers do different things?

- Present your defensive strategy to the rest of the class for a Speaking and Listening assessment.

- Now read Chapter 4, which includes the account of what actually happened during the Battle of the Cowshed. How did your plan compare? What does the battle tell you about the characters of Boxer, Snowball and Mollie?

TROUBLE ON THE FARM

The first sign of trouble at Animal Farm in Chapter 5 is to do with Mollie.

- Think back or look at your notes about Mollie. Was she ever very happy at the farm? Why do you think this was?

- Read the first page of Chapter 5 from 'As winter drew on, Mollie became more and more troublesome' to 'Three days later Mollie disappeared' and write the newspaper story to go with this event.

MOLLIE IS A TRAITOR

HELP

The **headline** should give an outline or indication of the whole story. Select your words carefully to give the right tone for the article.

The **article** in the first paragraph should expand details to help explain the headline. The second paragraph then adds further details, and so on through the first half of the article. All details relevant to the story must be included in the first half of the article.

The second half of the article gives information which is not necessarily part of the story such as interviews with eyewitnesses, friends or experts. Links with other stories or the previous day of the current story are often included at this stage. There are **human interest** elements.

Photographs to accompany the story are either taken at the time or, if this was not possible, a photograph from the newspaper's library may be included.

A **caption** written underneath the photograph explains the content using quite simple language.

The second sign of trouble is the driving away of Snowball. Read the rest of Chapter 5 and then look closely at the following two extracts.

Until now the animals had been about equally divided in their sympathies, but in a moment Snowball's eloquence had carried them away. In glowing sentences he painted a picture of Animal Farm as it might be when sordid labour was lifted from the animals' backs. His imagination had now run far beyond chaff-cutters and turnip-slicers. Electricity, he said, could operate threshing machines, ploughs, harrows, rollers and reapers and binders, besides supplying every stall with its own electric light, hot and cold water, and an electric heater. By the time he had finished speaking, there was no doubt as to which way the vote would go. But just at this moment Napoleon stood up and, casting a peculiar sidelong look at Snowball, uttered a high-pitched whimper of a kind no one had ever heard him utter before.

At this there was a terrible baying sound outside, and nine enormous dogs wearing brass-studded collars came bounding into the barn. They dashed straight for Snowball, who only sprang from his place just in time to escape their snapping jaws. In a moment he was out of the door and they were after him. Too amazed and frightened to speak, all the animals crowded through the door to watch the chase. Snowball was racing across the long pasture that led to the road. He was running as only a pig can run, but the dogs were close on his heels. Suddenly he slipped and it seemed certain that they had him. Then he was up again, running faster than ever, then the dogs were gaining on him again. One of them all but closed his jaws on Snowball's tail, but Snowball whisked it free just in time. Then he put on an extra spurt and, with a few inches to spare, slipped through a hole in the hedge and was seen no more.

Napoleon, with the dogs following him, now mounted onto the raised portion of the floor where Major had previously stood to deliver his speech. He announced that from now on the Sunday-morning Meetings would come to an end. They were unnecessary, he said, and wasted time. In future all questions relating to the working of the farm would be settled by a special committee of pigs, presided over by himself. These would meet in private and afterwards communicate their decisions to the others. The animals would still assemble on Sunday mornings to salute the flag, sing 'Beasts of England' and receive their orders for the week; but there would be no more debates.

- What argument does Snowball use to persuade the other animals?

- *'There was no doubt as to which way the vote would go'.* Which way was the vote going to go?

- Why has Napoleon trained the dogs in this way?

- Do you think Napoleon wanted to chase Snowball away or to have him killed? Why?

- What do you think this episode reveals about how some people gain and hold on to power?

- How do Napoleon's plans conflict with the life envisaged and promoted by Old Major at the beginning of the novel?

THE FIRST WINDMILL

Read Chapter 6. Look carefully at the section which explains how the animals build the windmill ('The windmill presented unexpected difficulties' to '...he would go alone to the quarry, collect a load of broken stone, and drag it down to the site of the windmill unassisted.').

- The animals struggle to build the windmill only for it to be ruined. Is it ruined by Snowball or the storm? What do you think happened to the windmill?

- Why is Napoleon eager to blame Snowball?

CHANGING THE COMMANDMENTS

- Look back at the original seven commandments in Chapter 2. Write them down leaving enough space to make notes about each one.

- *'Comrades, here and now I pronounce the death sentence upon Snowball.'* Which commandment(s) does this proclamation go against? Record what has happened on the farm which seems to go against some of the commandments.

- Write down the changed wording for any of these commandments. For example:

All animals are equal.

But the pigs take all of the milk and the apples.

The pigs manage the work, they don't actually do any physical work themselves.

The pigs make all decisions about the farm.

Dogs are trained by Napoleon to chase off his rival, Snowball. They are Napoleon's bodyguards.

Debates involving all the animals are stopped.

Napoleon becomes the leader.

- Up-date these notes as you continue reading the novel.

RE-WRITING HISTORY

Read Chapter 7. Snowball becomes the scapegoat for everything which goes wrong on the farm – even those things which would be impossible. In order to completely discredit him Napoleon sets about discrediting his actions during the Battle of the Cowshed. Read carefully Squealer's account of Snowball's actions during the Battle of the Cowshed from 'We had thought that Snowball's rebellion was caused by his vanity and ambition' to '...long before the Rebellion was ever thought of.'

- Write a paragraph explaining Squealer's version of the Battle of the Cowshed.
- Now re-read the account of the battle in Chapter 4. How do the two accounts differ? Write a detailed description of how Squealer has altered the events.

'NO ANIMAL SHALL KILL ANY OTHER ANIMAL.'

This chapter is very important because of the changes in life on Animal Farm. Napoleon is powerful because he is the acknowledged leader and is surrounded by very powerful dogs who obey only him. He uses this power to kill animals who are, or could become, troublemakers. Why does he select particular animals for slaughter? Why is Boxer one of them, although he foils their attack this time?

Imagine you are one of the minor animals. Write about this **purge** first making notes about the actual events. Decide who you are going to write as and consider the thoughts and emotions of the witnesses to this terrible happening. Start your writing '*I was there in the yard . . .*'

To **purge** is to clear something of unwanted things or to clear, for example a political party, of people who are thought not to be loyal to it.

FORMS OF REGIME

Anarchy – absence or failure of government

Autonomy – self-government

Democracy – a form of government in which the people have power freely to elect representatives to carry out the role of government

Dictatorship – governed by an all-powerful ruler who has absolute authority

Totalitarian – a system of government in which one party rules and allows no rivals

1 Has life on Animal Farm moved from one of these systems to another during the section of the novel you have read?

- What form of government was the farm under during Mr Jones's time there?

- After the formation of the commandments, what was the form of government? Did this change once the pigs took more control?

- What system of government has a supreme ruler?

- Describe how the system of government changes at Animal Farm. Refer to specific examples and events in order to support your points.

2 Can you predict what life on the farm is going to be like at the end of the novel? With a partner discuss what has happened so far and explore the possibilities for the future. You might find it useful to remind yourself of Old Major's dream and life under Mr Jones as a starting point. If you were one of the pigs, or Napoleon in particular, who would you find a nuisance? Is there any animal you would like to be rid of? Has anyone annoyed you so much perhaps you might think they deserve punishment?

NAPOLEON: FRIEND OF THE FATHERLESS

Now read Chapter 8. In this chapter Minimus writes a poem about Napoleon.
Look at the poem carefully and then complete the tasks below.

Friend of the fatherless!
Fountain of happiness!
Lord of the swill-bucket! Oh, how my soul is on
Fire when I gaze at thy
Calm and commanding eye,
Like the sun in the sky,
Comrade Napoleon!

Thou art the giver of
All that thy creatures love,
Full belly twice a day, clean straw to roll upon;
Every beast great or small
Sleeps at peace in his stall,
Thou watchest over all,
Comrade Napoleon!

Had I a sucking-pig,
Ere he had grown as big
Even as a pint bottle or as a rolling-pin,
He should have learned to be
Faithful and true to thee,
Yes, his first squeak should be
Comrade Napoleon!

- What is Minimus saying Napoleon is like in this poem? How much of the detail is strictly correct at this point in the novel?

- What is George Orwell saying Napoleon is like? What is he saying about the way in which Animal Farm is ruled now?

- Look closely at the vocabulary used in the poem and compare it with that used in 'Beasts of England' in Chapter 1. Orwell has used similar images but in a very different way. What effect does this have?

- Write a fourth stanza to Minimus's poem. You will need to think about it in two ways:

a As Minimus – how do you want to influence the animals' opinion of Napoleon?

b As Orwell – how do you want your readers to react to the poem? Will they believe everything you say?

THE SECOND WINDMILL

The building of the windmill and the trade with either Pilkington or Frederick for the timber are two linked events in the plot. Trace the history of the windmill from the time Snowball first mentions his plan in Chapter 5 to its final destruction in Chapter 8. Why is the windmill so important a) to their life on the farm b) to the way the farm is seen by others in the area? Why is trading the timber important to this venture?

The dramatic explosion of the windmill gives the animals courage to fight the well-armed attackers from Frederick's farm. Read the description of the victory celebration of the battle and make notes on the events and who does what.

They had won, but they were weary and bleeding. Slowly they began to limp back towards the farm. The sight of their dead comrades stretched upon the grass moved some of them to tears. And for a little while they halted in sorrowful silence at the place where the windmill had once stood. Yes, it was gone; almost the last trace of their labour was gone! Even the foundations were partially destroyed. And in rebuilding it they could not this time, as before, make use of the fallen stones. This time the stones had vanished too. The force of the explosion had flung them to distances of hundreds of yards. It was as though the windmill had never been.

As they approached the farm Squealer, who had unaccountably been absent during the fighting, came skipping towards them, whisking his tail and beaming with satisfaction. And the animals heard, from the direction of the farm buildings, the solemn booming of a gun.

'What is that gun firing for?' said Boxer.

'To celebrate our victory!' cried Squealer.

'What victory?' said Boxer. His knees were bleeding, he had lost a shoe and split his hoof, and a dozen pellets had lodged themselves in his hindleg.

'What victory, comrade? Have we not driven the enemy off our soil – the sacred soil of Animal Farm?'

'But they have destroyed the windmill. And we had worked on it for two years!'

'What matter? We will build another windmill. We will build six windmills if we feel like it. You do not appreciate, comrade, the mighty thing that we have done. The enemy was in occupation of this very ground that we stand upon. And now – thanks to the leadership of Comrade Napoleon – we have won every inch of it back again!'

'Then we have won back what we had before,' said Boxer.

'That is our victory,' said Squealer.

They limped into the yard. The pellets under the skin of Boxer's leg smarted painfully. He saw ahead of him the heavy labour of rebuilding the windmill from the foundations, and already in imagination he braced himself for the task. But for the first time it occurred to him that he was eleven years old and that perhaps his great muscles were not quite what they had once been.

But when the animals saw the green flag flying, and heard the gun firing again – seven times it was fired in all – and heard the speech that Napoleon made, congratulating them on their conduct, it did seem to them after all that they had won a great victory. The animals slain in the battle were given a solemn funeral. Boxer and Clover pulled the wagon which served as a hearse, and Napoleon himself walked at the head of the procession. Two whole days were given over to celebrations. There were songs, speeches, and more firing of the gun, and a special gift of an apple was bestowed on every animal, with two ounces of corn for each bird and three biscuits for each dog. It was announced that the battle would be called the Battle of the Windmill, and that Napoleon had created a new decoration, the Order of the Green Banner, which he had conferred upon himself. In the general rejoicings the unfortunate affair of the bank-notes was forgotten.

Write a storyboard for this section of the chapter using a layout like the one below.

'they halted in sorrowful silence
where the windmill had once stood'

'Napoleon had created a new decoration,
the Order of the Green Banner, which he
had conferred upon himself'

- You might like to consider how you would convey the following points to your audience:

  How Boxer feels

  How Squealer feels

  The atmosphere of rejoicing and celebration

  The effect the sounding of the gun has

  The awarding of the 'Order of the Green Banner'

  The banknotes . . .

- Do you consider the Battle of the Windmill to be a victory? If not, why not? How is it different to the victory of the Battle of the Cowshed?

HELP

A storyboard is a media technique to show, by sketching in a frame to represent a camera shot, what would be seen on the TV or film screen.

Along with these sketches, a storyboard notes the sounds and camera techniques required for each shot.

BOXER

Now read Chapter 9. What happens to Boxer in this chapter is one of the most important moments in the novel. Old Major's dream of a 'golden future time' has gradually changed into something very different.

- Boxer is used by George Orwell to represent certain qualities such as hard work, determination, simplicity and trustworthiness. Look back through the novel and make a list of Boxer's achievements.

- Use your list to prepare a citation. This is a formal document (rather like a certificate) which lists Boxer's qualities and achievements. Remember to use appropriate formal language, and to include details of Boxer's life and contribution to Animal Farm.

'THEY'RE TAKING BOXER AWAY!'

Read carefully the account of Boxer's removal from the farm from 'The animals were all at work weeding turnips under the supervision of a pig' to... "Boxer!' cried Clover in a terrible voice. 'Boxer! Get out! Get out quickly! They are taking you to your death!''.

There are different ways of interpreting the significance of Boxer's death in the context of the story as a whole. With a partner, consider and discuss each of the following possible interpretations.

Boxer's death shows that the pigs are totally corrupt and have destroyed Old Major's dream.

Orwell makes us feel angry with Boxer, for allowing himself to be exploited so ruthlessly by the pigs, without ever complaining or even realising!

Boxer's death, and Squealer's false account of it, show how easily the other animals can be misled and will believe anything they are told.

Orwell makes us feel sorry for Boxer because his life ends so sadly.

Boxer is a noble creature. His ignoble death will inspire the other animals to 'wake up' and see what is happening to them – they might now rebel against the pigs.

His death reveals the weakness and stupidity of all the animals who are unfit to run their own lives.

Boxer represents the ordinary worker who fails to recognise that he is downtrodden and exploited by those in positions of power.

- Can you think of any other possible ways of interpreting Boxer's death and the way that George Orwell describes it?

- In pairs, or small groups, select one interpretation. Using evidence from elsewhere in the novel, prepare and deliver an argument which supports this viewpoint. Listen carefully to the other arguments. Can you agree on which interpretations are most valid? Are they all equally valid or are some more valid than others?!

Now read from Chapter 10 to the final chapter of *Animal Farm*. Look carefully at the two extracts below.

A week later, in the afternoon, a number of dog-carts drove up to the farm. A deputation of neighbouring farmers, had been invited to make a tour of inspection. They were shown all over the farm, and expressed great admiration for everything they saw, especially the windmill. The animals were weeding the turnip field. They worked diligently, hardly raising their faces from the ground, and not knowing whether to be more frightened of the pigs or of the human visitors.

Later Mr Pilkington says to the gathered group of local farmers and pigs:

Today he and his friends had visited Animal Farm and inspected every inch of it with their own eyes, and what did they find? Not only the most up-to-date methods, but a discipline and an orderliness which should be an example to all farmers everywhere. He believed he was right in saying that the lower animals on Animal Farm did more work and received less food than any animals in the country. Indeed, he and his fellow-visitors today observed many features which they intended to introduce on their own farms immediately.

- What did the visitors see on their inch-by-inch tour of Animal Farm? You have now read all of the novel. What do you imagine the farm to look like? Where do the animals live? What is it like for the pigs inside the house?

- Script the scene of the conducted tour of the farm. Include a variety of speaking parts for the farmers and the pigs of Animal Farm. Try to include details about:

  the way the pigs organise the other animals

  working conditions for the other animals

  what the farmers were expecting and what the farm is actually like

  things the farmers might try to introduce on their own farms

  stage directions which give an idea of the farm layout, buildings and fields

  stage directions which indicate the thoughts and feelings of the characters.

- In Chapter 1 Old Major says of their life on Animal Farm:

  'Let us face it: our lives are miserable, laborious, and short. We are born, we are given just so much food as will keep the breath in our bodies, and those of us who are capable of it are forced to work to the last atom of our strength, and the very instant that our usefulness has come to an end we are slaughtered with hideous cruelty.'

  How has old Major's dream changed?

- 'All animals are equal but some animals are more equal than others'. The commandments and their changes clearly demonstrate the power changes on Animal Farm during the course of the novel. Explore the changes in the commandments and show how power is transferred through the process.

NAPOLEON: SUPREME RULER OF ANIMAL FARM

Animal Farm is also a success story. Napoleon is very powerful by the end of the novel having risen from the ranks as just another pig in the rebellion against Mr Jones. Slowly he asserts his cleverness and takes control of the farm. Once the pigs are established as leaders he becomes the dominant pig in that elite group. Challengers are dismissed and the populace is kept under control through terror. His moment of honour comes when he is proclaimed Supreme Ruler. The world has not been short of revolutionaries and dictators, but here are two recent examples.

Guevara, Che (1928–67) Latin American guerrilla leader and revolutionary who believed that violent revolution was the only solution to Latin America's social and political inequalities. Although born into a middle-class Argentinian family, he relinquished his privileged upbringing and education to join Cuban revolutionary Fidel Castro in his fight against Cuban dictator Fulgencio Batista in the 1950s, and served as Cuba's Minister of Industry when Castro seized power in 1961. Guevara believed passionately in peasant-based revolutionary movements and wrote two books about guerrilla warfare. He left Cuba in 1965 to join a terrorist/revolutionary movement in Bolivia, and was captured and shot by the Bolivian army on October 9, 1967. Che Guevara remains an icon of the revolutionary left and his life is often cited as an example of heroic, uncorrupted revolutionary idealism on behalf of all dispossessed peoples.

Quaddafi, Musammar al- (1924–) Libyan revolutionary leader, he came to power in 1969 after a coup in which Quaddafi overthrew King Idris I and proclaimed Libya as an Arab republic. Once in power, he made himself chairman of the Revolutionary Command Council. He has remained in power as a result of a combination of dictatorial powers and personal charisma, as well as being bolstered by Libya's vast oil wealth. He launched a cultural and social revolution that transformed Libyan society into a fundamentalist Islamic state. In 1977 he established what he called jamahiriyah ('state of the masses') and in 1979 gave up all formal posts in the administration whilst continuing to remain as the country's leader and figurehead. He is widely regarded in the West as the main financier of international terrorism and was injured, and his young daughter killed, as a result of US bombing of Libyan targets following a terrorist incident traced to Libya in April 1986.

Write a similar account about Napoleon for inclusion in a reference book or CD.

THE RUSSIAN CONNECTION

Writing an allegory allows Orwell to put forward his views about things happening in the world around him. *Animal Farm* was intended to comment on the events in Russia during the period between the Revolution in 1917 and the end of the Second World War.

Can you match the events in Russian history to the events in the plot of *Animal Farm*? The sequence of events of *Animal Farm* are in the correct order whilst those of Russian history are randomly identified by letters of the alphabet. Refer to the Help Box opposite for some clues.

ANIMAL FARM

1 Old Major tells the animals of his dream of a new life, free from Jones who is cruel, inefficient and drunk.

2 Animals take over the farm and drive Jones and his wife away.

3 Napoleon and Snowball lead the animals. The seven commandments are painted on the barn.

4 Animals are educated. Napoleon takes control of the puppies.

5 Battle of the Cowshed – when Jones and men from the neighbouring farms try to get the farm back.

6 Napoleon gives orders and tells animals what to do.

7 Napoleon uses dogs to chase Snowball from the farm.

8 Plans to build a windmill fail. The windmill is destroyed.

9 Napoleon circulates false stories about what Snowball has done.

10 Animals are hungry – there is a lack of food on the farm.

11 Animals who do not support Animalism are put on trial and killed.

12 Napoleon is seen less and only appears on special occasions. He is god-like.

13 Napoleon plays farmer Frederick and farmer Pilkington against each other. Timber is eventually sold to farmer Frederick.

14 Farmer Frederick blows up the re-built windmill.

15 The Battle of the Windmill when the animals chase off farmer Frederick.

16 Death of Boxer.

17 Pigs behave as humans and celebrate with local farmers.

18 Pigs and local farmers begin to fall out.

RUSSIAN HISTORY

A Tsar Nicholas II was stern and repressive. He believed in his divine right to rule.

B Stalin used secret police to get rid of rivals including Trotsky in 1927.

C Famine in Russia.

D The ideal of hard work to solve all problems was shown to be false.

E Germany invaded Russia 1941.

F Stalin and Trotsky were Russian leaders. There were lots of slogans about Communism.

G Stalin had purges and show trials, when people who didn't agree with him were punished and killed.

H Russia had disagreements with America and Britain.

I Stalin first arranged to be an ally of Britain and France against Germany but then made an agreement with Germany instead in 1939.

J Communists seized power in October Revolution 1917. The Tsar and his family were killed.

K Stalin became distant and encouraged his followers to 'worship' him.

L Civil war 1918 when western countries tried to help on the side against the communists.

M The Russian leaders had absolute power. Stalin met with America and Britain to discuss the war, 1943.

N Russians fought with courage and endurance and drove Germany out of Russia in 1943.

O Propaganda about external enemies helped the leaders to keep control of Russia.

P People were educated to think differently from before. Russian leaders established control of the secret police.

Q Stalin's dictatorship.

R Five Year Plan to improve Russia failed (1928–32).

HELP

Old Major = Marx/Lenin
Jones = Tsar Nicholas II
Napoleon = Stalin
Snowball = Trotsky

Dogs = Secret police
Frederick = Germany
Pilkington = Britain
Boxer = Russian workers

- Look back to the explanation of an allegory at the beginning of this book. What do you think Orwell was trying to say about Russia? Write this as a speech which Orwell might have made or as an interview with questions and answers.

- In what ways did Orwell expose the Soviet Myth? Think carefully about why he might have chosen to write *Animal Farm* as an allegory. What would have happened if he had just recorded the bold truth? Would the book have become famous and would you be reading it now?

DIFFERENT SOCIETIES

The word **utopia** comes from the Greek *outopia* meaning 'no place' and is a pun on *eutopia* meaning 'good place'. In 1516 Sir Thomas More wrote a famous book called *Utopia* describing an imaginary and perfect commonwealth where all people were educated and worked, where all land was owned by society and all religions were tolerated. The word **utopia** has now come to mean any fictional and imaginary world which is better than our own. In *Animal Farm* Old Major's dream pictures a modern-day utopia where the animals will be free from suffering and indignity in a society which cares for them all and in which they can all work for the benefit of their society.

Dystopia is the opposite of utopia (from the Greek meaning 'bad place'). It means an imaginary world which is unpleasant, for example where society is run to support the well-being of only a few powerful people. George Orwell also wrote a book called *Nineteen Eighty-Four*. It was written in 1948: Orwell turned the last two numbers of the date around and imagined what society might be like in the future. He pictured a dystopia where society was totalitarian (look back to page 22) and run by a police state. You may like to read this novel to learn more about dystopia and Orwell's writing.

- Can you think of any other dystopias from books you have read or films you have seen, for example 'Waterworld' and 'Terminator'? What are the features of these types of society?

EXTENSION AND REVISION TASKS

The following tasks will give you opportunities to revise and develop what you have learned in this book.

- Working with a partner, take it in turns to re-tell the story of *Animal Farm*. To help you, turn the story into 10 key events. Try to retell it as a one-minute, two-minute or five-minute story. Can you write a 100, 200 or 500 word version of the story?

- List the main characters in the story and write next to them what events each of these is involved with during the story. Check your characters with someone else and make any changes that are necessary.

- Which characters does each of these words refer to?

  loyal awkward vain cruel strong devious powerful innocent protective manipulative lazy clever selfish dishonest serious silly

- There are optimistic and pessimistic events in the novel. Work through your plot summary giving each event a + for optimistic or a − for pessimistic. Select one of each and look carefully at the relevant section of the novel. How has Orwell conveyed these feelings to the reader? Make detailed notes, concentrating on the language and structure of the writing.

- Construct a chart or graph which shows, in the right sequence, how events move back and forth from positive (optimism) to negative (pessimism) throughout the novel. Use the example given below to start you off:

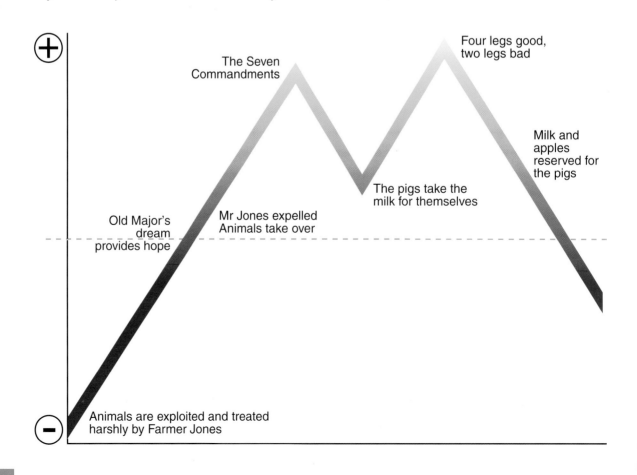